W9-CCT-934

COMPREHENSIVE RESEARCH
AND STUDY GUIDE

BLOOM'S
MAJOR
SHORT
STORY
WRITERS

O. Henry

EDITED AND WITH AN
INTRODUCTION BY HAROLD BLOOM

BLOOM'S MAJOR DRAMATISTS

Anton Chekhov
Henrik Ibsen
Arthur Miller
Eugene O'Neill
Shakespeare's Comedies
Shakespeare's Histories
Shakespeare's Romances
Shakespeare's Tragedies
George Bernard Shaw
Tennessee Williams

BLOOM'S MAJOR NOVELISTS

Jane Austen
The Brontës
Willa Cather
Charles Dickens
William Faulkner
F. Scott Fitzgerald
Nathaniel Hawthorne
Ernest Hemingway
Toni Morrison
John Steinbeck
Mark Twain
Alice Walker

BLOOM'S MAJOR SHORT STORY WRITERS

William Faulkner
F. Scott Fitzgerald
Ernest Hemingway
O. Henry
James Joyce
Herman Melville
Flannery O'Connor
Edgar Allan Poe
J. D. Salinger
John Steinbeck
Mark Twain
Eudora Welty

BLOOM'S MAJOR WORLD POETS

Geoffrey Chaucer
Emily Dickinson
John Donne
T. S. Eliot
Robert Frost
Langston Hughes
John Milton
Edgar Allan Poe
Shakespeare's Poems & Sonnets
Alfred, Lord Tennyson
Walt Whitman
William Wordsworth

BLOOM'S NOTES

The Adventures of Huckleberry Finn
Aeneid
The Age of Innocence
Animal Farm
The Autobiography of Malcolm X
The Awakening
Beloved
Beowulf
Billy Budd, Benito Cereno, & Bartleby the Scrivener
Brave New World
The Catcher in the Rye
Crime and Punishment
The Crucible

Death of a Salesman
A Farewell to Arms
Frankenstein
The Grapes of Wrath
Great Expectations
The Great Gatsby
Gulliver's Travels
Hamlet
Heart of Darkness & The Secret Sharer
Henry IV, Part One
I Know Why the Caged Bird Sings
Iliad
Inferno
Invisible Man
Jane Eyre
Julius Caesar

King Lear
Lord of the Flies
Macbeth
A Midsummer Night's Dream
Moby-Dick
Native Son
Nineteen Eighty-Four
Odyssey
Oedipus Plays
Of Mice and Men
The Old Man and the Sea
Othello
Paradise Lost
A Portrait of the Artist as a Young Man
The Portrait of a Lady

Pride and Prejudice
The Red Badge of Courage
Romeo and Juliet
The Scarlet Letter
Silas Marner
The Sound and the Fury
The Sun Also Rises
A Tale of Two Cities
Tess of the D'Urbervilles
Their Eyes Were Watching God
To Kill a Mockingbird
Uncle Tom's Cabin
Wuthering Heights

COMPREHENSIVE RESEARCH
AND STUDY GUIDE

BLOOM'S
MAJOR
SHORT STORY
WRITERS

O. Henry

EDITED AND WITH AN INTRODUCTION BY HAROLD BLOOM

© 1999 by Chelsea House Publishers, a division of Main Line Book Co.

Introduction © 1999 by Harold Bloom

Printed and bound in the United States of America.

3 5 7 9 8 6 4 2

Library of Congress Cataloging-in-Publication Data

O. Henry / edited and with an introduction by Harold Bloom.
p.   cm. – (Bloom's major short story writers)
Includes bibliographical references and index.
ISBN 0-7910-5123-4 (hardcover)
1. Henry, O., 1862-1910—Criticism and interpretation—Handbooks,
Manuals, etc.   2. Henry, O., 1862-1910—Examinations—Study guides.
3. Short story—Examinations—Study guides.   4. Short story—
Handbooks, manuals, etc.
I. Bloom, Harold.   II. Title.   III. Series.
PS2649.P5Z68   1998
813'.54—dc21
98-37753
CIP

Chelsea House Publishers
1974 Sproul Road, Suite 400
Broomall, PA 19008-0914

CONTRIBUTING EDITOR: Aaron Tillman

Contents

User's Guide

This volume is designed to present biographical, critical, and biblio-graphical information on the author's best-known or most important short stories. Following Harold Bloom's editor's note and introduction are a detailed biography of the author, discussing major life events and important literary accomplishments. A plot summary of each short story follows, tracing significant themes, patterns, and motifs in the work, and an annotated list of characters supplies brief information on the main characters in each story.

A selection of critical extracts, derived from previously published mate-rial from leading critics, analyzes aspects of each short story. The extracts consist of statements from the author, if available, early reviews of the work, and later evaluations up to the present. A bibliography of the author's writings (including a complete list of all books written, cowritten, edited, and translated), a list of additional books and articles on the author and the work, and an index of themes and ideas in the author's writings conclude the volume.

~

Harold Bloom is Sterling Professor of the Humanities at Yale University and Henry W. and Albert A. Berg Professor of English at the New York University Graduate School. He is the author of over 20 books and the editor of more than 30 anthologies of literary criticism.

Professor Bloom's works include *Shelley's Mythmaking* (1959), *The Visionary Company* (1961), *Blake's Apocalypse* (1963), *Yeats* (1970), *A Map of Misreading* (1975), *Kabbalah and Criticism* (1975), and *Agon: Toward a Theory of Revisionism* (1982). *The Anxiety of Influence* (1973) sets forth Professor Bloom's provocative theory of the literary relation-ships between the great writers and their predecessors. His most recent books include *The American Religion* (1992), *The Western Canon* (1994), *Omens of Millennium: The Gnosis of Angels, Dreams, and Resur-rection* (1996), and *Shakespeare: The Invention of the Human* (1998).

Professor Bloom earned his Ph.D. from Yale University in 1955 and has served on the Yale faculty since then. He is a 1985 MacArthur Founda-tion Award recipient and served as the Charles Eliot Norton Professor of Poetry at Harvard University in 1987-88. He is currently the editor of other Chelsea House series in literary criticism, including BLOOM'S NOTES, BLOOM'S MAJOR POETS, MAJOR LITERARY CHARACTERS, MODERN CRITICAL VIEWS, MODERN CRITICAL INTERPRETATIONS, and WOMEN WRITERS OF ENGLISH AND THEIR WORKS.

Editor's Note

My Introduction contrasts the wistful sentimentality of "The Gift of the Magi" with the darker vision of "A Municipal Report" and "The Furnished Room."

Critical views on "The Gift of the Magi" begin with Hyder E. Rollins, who deprecates O. Henry's fondness for surprise double-endings. E. Hudson Long contextualizes the story in William Sydney Porter's life, while Eugene Current-Garcia celebrates the mingled motives of the tale.

William Saroyan, a popular story writer in O. Henry's tradition, gives an account of his first reading of "The Gift of the Magi," after which Willis Wager comments on the tale's style, and Richard O'Connor gives the exact background to the plot.

Fantasy is emphasized by Philip Stevnick, while Trueman E. O'Quinn returns us to Porter's biography and its sorrows. Karen Charmaine Blansfield outlines the formulaic elements in O. Henry's art.

"A Municipal Report," as noted by Fred Lewis Pattee, reflects the naturalistic influence of the novelist Frank Norris. The names in the story are commented on by Robert H. Davis and Arthur B. Maurice, while E. Hudson Long relates "A Municipal Report" to O. Henry's declining health during the final year of his life.

The Southern literary tradition is invoked by Eugene Current-Garcia, after which other aspects of regionalism are detailed by E. Hudson Long. Richard O'Connor discusses the reception of O'Henry's last volume, while C. Alphonso Smith returns us to the challenge of Frank Norris, and Eugene Current-Garcia to the achieved narrative tone of "A Municipal Report."

"The Furnished Room," O. Henry's somber masterpiece, is praised for its popular appeal by Robert H. Davis and Arthur B. Maurice, and also lauded by the eminent scholar George F. Whicher.

The imagistic strength of the story is analyzed by Van Wyck Brooks and Otto L. Bettmann, after which Gilbert Millstein comments upon O. Henry's knowingness, as a New Yorker. Roman Samarin, a Russian scholar, defends the story's realism, while David Stuart considers its biographical background.

Introduction

HAROLD BLOOM

William Sydney Porter is a central figure in American popular literature. He has a huge, permanent audience, and is all but identified with the short story as a genre, though he cannot be considered one of its inventors, or indeed one of its crucial innovators. His comic gifts are considerable though limited, and his careful naturalism is almost always shadowed by that of his precursor, Frank Norris. What matters most about O. Henry is the audience he has maintained for a century: ordinary readers who find themselves in his stories, not more truly and more strange, but rather as they were and are.

O. Henry's most famous tale, "The Gift of the Magi," always survives its palpable sentimentalities. The author, lovingly interested in characters founded upon his wife and himself, presents them with delicacy and compassion. Love, Dr. Samuel Johnson observed, was the wisdom of fools and the folly of the wise. That would be an admirable critical perception of Shakespeare's *King Lear* but is too grand and fierce for the gentle "Gift of the Magi," where the foolishness of love pragmatically manifests itself as a wisdom.

A more complete vision is manifested in "A Municipal Report," one of O. Henry's most complex stories: humorous, paradoxical, even a touch Borgesian in the personality of Azalea Adair, a survival of the Old South. Though the author attempts a dispassionate stance, he clearly is glad, as we are, when Azalea Adair's exploiter, the dreadful Major Wentworth Caswell, is discovered dead on a dark street:

> The gentle citizens who had known him stood about and searched
> their vocabularies to find some good words, if it were possible, to speak
> of him. One kind-looking man said, after much thought: 'When "Cas"
> was about fo'teen he was one of the best spellers in school.'

"The Furnished Room," very late O. Henry, may be the darkest of all his stories. Coincidence, almost invariably overworked by the author, becomes something like a fatality here. The double suicide of lovers is made plausible by all the griminess of urban decay. A single sentence, describing a stair carpet, catches memorably the fetid atmosphere of the rooming-house, in which both lovers have died, or will die:

> It seemed to have become vegetable, to have degenerated in that rank, sunless air to lush lichen or spreading moss that grew in patches to the staircase and was viscid under the foot like organic matter.

This stands between the luxuriant rankness of Tennyson's *Maud* and certain Tennysonian effects in early T.S. Eliot and in Faulkner. A populist in his art, O. Henry had a repressed Symbolist poet in his spirit, and this ghostly presence helps to temper the too-evident surprises of his work. ❀

Biography of
William Sydney Porter ("O. Henry")

(1862–1910)

William Sydney Porter was born on September 11, 1862, in Greensboro, North Carolina, the second son of Dr. Algernon Sidney and Mary Jane Porter. William's mother died three years after his birth, and he, along with his father and brother, moved in with his maternal grandmother and his aunt Lina. Porter credited Aunt Lina with developing his interest in literature and art through her regular tutoring sessions.

Porter began his working career at age 17 as a pharmacist apprentice in his uncle Clark's drugstore. Two years later he received his license to practice pharmacy from the North Carolina Pharmaceutical Association. Porter worked as a pharmacist for slightly over a year before leaving for southwest Texas, where he became a house guest of Mr. and Mrs. Richard Hall. For two years he worked on the Hall cattle ranch in La Salle County, Texas. Here he began writing humorous anecdotal letters and drawing comic strips. In 1884, he moved to Austin, Texas, where he met Athol Estes, whom he married three years later. In 1888 Athol gave birth to a son, who died shortly after birth. Their second child, Margaret, was born later that year, after which Athol became seriously ill.

In 1891, Porter lost his job at the Texas Land Office and became a teller in the First National Bank of Austin. While still working at the bank, he started the publication *The Rolling Stone*, a humor weekly. The magazine went out of print a year later, at which time he was also fired by the bank and indicted for embezzlement. The case was closed in 1895 only to be reopened the following year.

Porter was arrested in Houston in February 1896. On his way to stand trial in Austin, he fled to New Orleans and from there to Honduras. He returned to Texas in January 1897, however, to be with his dying wife. After her death Porter and his daughter, Margaret, moved into Athol's mother's house, where he awaited trial. During this residency, in December 1891, Porter's first story, "Miracle of Lava Canyon," was accepted for publication by McClure Company.

In February 1898, Porter was found guilty of embezzlement, and in April he began serving a five-year sentence at the federal penitentiary in Ohio. In prison he began a professional writing career, writing and publishing more than a dozen stories. He was released on good behavior after serving three years of his sentence.

William spent the following year living with his daughter in Pittsburgh and writing stories for the *Pittsburgh Dispatch*, as well as for various New York magazines. He moved to New York in 1902 where he gained immediate success writing under the pseudonym "O. Henry." He signed a contract for writing weekly feature short stories with the *New York Sunday World* in 1903, generating more than 100 stories within two years, and lifting O. Henry to national recognition.

O. Henry's first book, *Cabbages and Kings*, was published in 1904. The book was based largely on his experience in Honduras. In April 1906, he published *The Four Million*, a collection that included his most famous New York stories, which gained him international recognition. He married a childhood sweetheart, Sara Lindsay Coleman, in 1907, and in the ensuing three years, he published seven additional volumes of collected short stories.

William Sydney Porter, a.k.a. "O. Henry," died in New York on June 5, 1910, after a six-month illness. He was buried in Asheville, North Carolina.

Between 1910 and 1920, Doubleday and Company published five posthumous volumes of O. Henry stories and also released the first authorized biography of William Sydney Porter, which was written by C. Alphonso Smith. Since that time, O. Henry's works have been translated into various languages and have sold millions of copies, and many other biographies have been written about his life. ❀

Plot Summary of
"The Gift of the Magi"

"The Gift of the Magi," O. Henry's classic tale of selflessness and love, opens on Christmas Eve, with Mrs. Della Dillingham Young greatly distressed over the minuscule sum she has managed to save for her husband Jim's Christmas present. The reader is told of the great lengths to which Della has gone to obtain a mere one dollar and 87 cents. She falls onto her couch and weeps with uncontrolled abandon. While Della is sobbing, the reader is exposed to one of O. Henry's unique narrative asides, which in this case, comes in the form of a brief tour of Della and Jim's "$8 per week" flat, highlighting its cheap and ragged appearance. When Della's sob is over, the story continues.

Della makes herself presentable once again, and the reader is told of the hard times that Della and many common people of the day have had to endure. The narrative then moves back into a description of the home, before lingering between the windows of the room, where Della catches her reflection in a "pier-glass." At this point the reader is introduced to the two most valued possessions in the Dillingham Youngs' household: Della's long, beautiful hair and Jim's gold watch.

Della walks out to the street and stops next to a sign reading: MME. SOFRONIE. HAIR GOODS OF ALL KINDS. Della ascends the stairs to Mme. Sofronie's store to ask if she will buy Della's hair. The Madame offers twenty dollars for it, and Della quickly accepts.

Della spends the ensuing few hours searching the stores for a worthy present. Ultimately, she comes across the perfect gift: a platinum chain for Jim's prized watch. She buys the chain for 21 dollars, leaving her exactly 87 cents to spare, before she rushes home to fantasize about the glorious addition to Jim's watch. When she arrives back at her flat, she is struck by the realization that most of her hair is gone, and her appearance is considerably different. She spends the next 40 minutes curling and styling her hair, leaving her looking like a curly-haired boy. Realizing that little can be done, she turns her attention toward dinner preparations.

When Della hears Jim's footsteps, she recites a quick prayer, hoping that Jim's affection will remain. But Jim opens the door and greets Della with a completely blank expression. Della was unprepared for this and becomes fearful. She runs to Jim to explain why she has cut her hair, reassuring him that it will grow out again. Jim remains motionless in the doorway, scarcely acknowledging her. Della continues to reinforce the fact that she had to sell it in order to purchase an adequate present for him. She confesses her undying love for her husband and offers to serve him dinner.

Jim finally breaks out of his coma-like state and embraces his wife. The narrative then offers the couple some space to engage in their private act of affection: "For ten seconds let us regard with discreet scrutiny some inconsequential object in the other direction." This narrative aside, which is a distinct trademark of O. Henry, functions on a few levels: On one level, O. Henry calls attention to himself as a storyteller; on another level, it acts as a humorous moment to relieve the anxious circumstances of Jim's arrival; and on yet another level, it sustains the suspense of what ultimately will be revealed. O. Henry uses this aside to bring up, for the first time, the title relation: a quick mention about the gifts brought by the Magi. O. Henry assures the reader that this will be "illuminated later on."

Following their embrace, Jim removes a package from his overcoat and places it on the table. He pledges his deep devotion to his wife, indicating that she will understand his reaction once she opens his gift. Della tears open the package and is overcome with emotion at the sight of the lavish comb set Della had always dreamed of owning. Della reassures Jim once again that her hair grows very fast, before excitedly retrieving the present which she had purchased for him.

After seeing the platinum watch chain, Jim places it to the side, extends an ironic smile, and reveals that he has sold his watch for the money to buy the comb set. He goes on to suggest that they enjoy their dinner.

The narrator takes over for the final paragraph, recounting the tale of the Magi, the "wonderfully wise men—who brought gifts to the Babe in the manger." The narrator claims that the Magi initiated the tradition of exchanging Christmas presents, recognizing Della and Jim Dillingham Young as representatives of the true qualities of the Magi.

"The Gift of the Magi" is O. Henry's most famous piece. It is a rich story, offering a valuable look at his unique narrative method, while also providing the "surprise ending," a trademark of his work. ❀

List of Characters in
"The Gift of the Magi"

Mrs. Della Dillingham Young is the first character the reader encounters. She is distressed over the inadequate sum she has saved to buy a Christmas present for her husband. She decides to sell her precious, long hair to obtain the money she needs to buy a platinum chain for her husband's gold watch. When the gifts are exchanged, it is revealed that Della's husband has sold his watch in order to obtain the money needed to buy Della an extravagant comb set.

Mr. James Dillingham Young is Della's hard-working husband, who has had to adapt to his diminishing wages. Jim's gold watch, along with Della's hair, are the two truly valuable possessions remaining in the Dillingham Young household. Jim sells his watch to purchase a comb set for his wife. When he returns from work, he discovers that his wife has sold her hair to purchase a chain for his watch.

Madame Sofronie is the owner of a hair goods store. She purchases Della's hair for twenty dollars ❀

Critical Views on
"The Gift of the Magi"

HYDER E. ROLLINS ON O. HENRY'S CONCLUSIONS

[Hyder E. Rollins (1889–1958) was a professor at Harvard University and a contributor to many scholarly journals and research projects. He provided assistance to E. Hudson Long for his biography on O. Henry, entitled *O. Henry: The Man and His Work*. In this excerpt, Rollins discusses the "double-surprise" ending found in "The Gift of the Magi," claiming that O. Henry's continued use of this type of ending "grows tiresome."]

His conclusions—they are O. Henry's and no one else's. Children play "crack-the-whip," not for the fun of the long preliminary run, but for the excitement of the final sharp twist that throws them off their feet. So adults read O. Henry, impatiently wincing at the swiftly moving details in pleased expectancy of a surprising ending. The conclusion is an enigma: the author has your nerves all a-quiver until the last sentence. There are few explanations, the surprise comes quickly, and the story is finished. O. Henry is as much a master of the unexpected ending as Frank Stockton was of the insolvable ending, and one must admire his skill. For although these endings are unexpected, the author never makes any statement in the body that can be held against him. On the contrary, the body is a careful preparation for the dénouement, even if the most searching reader can seldom detect it. This is true even of the very poor story "Girl," in which O. Henry deliberately entraps the reader into believing that Hartley is imploring Vivienne to become his wife, when in reality, as we discover at the end of the story, he is imploring her to become his wife's cook. A few more stories like "Girl" would have ruined O. Henry's reputation. In "Thimble, Thimble" and several other stories he has adopted the conclusion made famous by "The Lady or the Tiger?" In all the others, the unexpected dénouement occurs, and in many of them are two distinct surprises that will shock the most phlegmatic reader to laughter. The most popular of the double-surprise stories is "The Gift of the Magi." But the continued use of the unexpected ending grows tiresome, and when one sits down and reads all or the greater part of the two hundred and forty-eight short stories, he feels that the biggest surprise O. Henry could have given him would have been a natural, expected ending. But it should be added that his surprise endings have none of the brutal cynicism which distinguishes de Maupassant's "Necklace" and Mérimée"'s "Mateo Falcone"; his endings, on the other hand, are genuinely humorous, genuinely sympathetic, and genuinely human.

—Hyder E. Rollins, "O. Henry," in *Sewanee Review* 22 (1914): pp. 225–26.

E. HUDSON LONG ON O. HENRY'S EXPERIENCES IN NEW ORLEANS AND THE TROPICS

[E. Hudson Long, an established scholar and educator, taught at Baylor University and has had various publications including a biography on O. Henry, entitled *O. Henry: The Man and His Work*. In this excerpt taken from that biography, Long creates a parallel between the actual events prior to his wife's death and the selflessness found in "The Gift of the Magi."]

At one time Porter confided to Jennings that he never intended to return to the States and was looking for a place to anchor safely. When he had found one and had located a suitable school for Margaret, he intended to send for his family. In the meantime he wrote regular letters back home, sometimes sending them to Louis Kreisle, who then delivered them to Athol. At other times the letters were sent to Mrs. Wilson in Houston, who remained anonymous, read-dressing and relaying them to Edd R. Smith in Austin, who handed them to Athol. The letters which Athol wrote to Porter in return were sent first to Houston, then to New Orleans, and from there to Honduras. In his letters, too, Porter expressed his desire to establish a home in the tropics, and disclosed that he did not spend all his time in the ease and conviviality pictured by Jennings. He wrote once that he had been digging ditches to earn a livelihood. Likewise he revealed there were times when he was without a place to stay or anything to eat save what he could forage. Mrs. Wilson has said that she herself received three letters from Porter while he was in Central America, one from Honduras, one from Puerto Cortes, and one from Trujillo.

Meanwhile Athol, in spite of her poor health and her parents' willingness to provide for her, wanted to earn something until Will could once again take care of her and Margaret. She started a course in business college but was unable to finish because her health failed under the strain. Persisting in her efforts, she made a point-lace handkerchief, which she sold for twenty-five dollars, and then, like Della in "The Gift of the Magi," spent the money for her husband's Christmas box. A month later, when Porter learned from Mrs. Roach that Athol, with a temperature of 105 degrees, had packed this box for him, he knew that she was dying. Abandoning all thought of a home in Honduras, he started back to Austin. He knew that if he returned there he would have to stand trial, but he had only one thought: to reach Athol before she died.

—E. Hudson Long, *O. Henry: The Man and His Work* (New York: A. S. Barnes and Company, 1949): pp. 86–88.

EUGENE CURRENT-GARCIA ON O. HENRY'S NEW YORK STORIES

[Eugene Current-Garcia is Hargis Professor Emeritus of American Literature at Auburn University. He helped found the *Southern Humanities Review* in 1967 and served as editor and co-editor until 1979. His publications include *What Is the Short Story?* and *American Short Stories Before 1850*. In this excerpt, Garcia explores the themes of joy and sadness in "The Gift of the Magi."]

"I would like to live a lifetime in each street in New York. Every house has a drama in it," O. Henry is reported to have said on one occasion. To understand what he meant by "drama" in this context, one would have to consider carefully two of the stories which, by common consent, still stand at the head of O. Henry favorites: "The Gift of the Magi" and "The Furnished Room." These represent the polar opposites of joy and sadness with which his imagination clothed the domestic life of average New Yorkers; and, though both may seem somewhat dated now, they still possess a strong popular appeal based on a universal yearning for an unattainable ideal. It is not surprising that "The Gift of the Magi" still enjoys such widespread fame, for in this trite little tale of mutual self-sacrifice between husband and wife, O. Henry crystallized dramatically what the world in all its stored-up wisdom knows to be of fundamental value in ordinary family life. Unselfish love shared, regardless of the attendant difficulties or distractions—this is the idea repeatedly implied as a criterion in his fictional treatment of domestic affairs. If such love is present, life can be a great adventure transcending all drabness; if it is absent, nothing else can take its place. Conversely, because it is often absent—or when present, it exists only momentarily and in a fragile state—the world can recognize and take to heart the grim meaning of life without it. O. Henry wrote few stories of ordinary family life that approach in tenderness and universal appeal the qualities found in "The Gift of the Magi"; and fewer still of those that match the bleakness of "The Furnished Room." But among the two dozen or so in which he attempted to dramatize the family life of the four million, perhaps seven or eight deserve and can stand comparison of these.

— Eugene Current-Garcia, *O. Henry* (*William Sydney Porter*) (Boston: Twayne Publishers, 1965): pp. 115–16.

WILLIAM SAROYAN ON O. HENRY AND THE LITTLE PEOPLE

[William Saroyan (1908–1981) was a prolific short story writer, playwright, and novelist. He received an American Book Award nomination in 1980 for *Obituaries*. His other publications include *Chance Meetings* (1978) and *Births* (1981). In this excerpt, Saroyan gives a humorous description of his first encounter with O. Henry's work, referring specifically to "The Gift of the Magi."]

Everybody wants to have something alive to call his own, to believe is *his* alone, to watch, to remember, to love, to worry about, to take pride in, to believe *needs* him. The story of the man who saves the life of the desperate girl who is about to commit suicide, and transforms her through love into a great and beautiful lady, is told again and again, as well as the story of the man who meets the girl who appears to be feeble-minded and transforms her into a profound thinker.

Most men, however, because of circumstances beyond their control (as we say), are not able to find such excellent material to love and transform.

No matter. Any man, any woman, any child—who has *got* to have something alive to make his own—can find something alive, can find it sometimes out of the air itself (such as a spider). But I'm not talking about a king in a cave watching a spider spin its web again and again and learning from this feat of perseverance to go back and beat hell out of his cousin or brother or mother or uncle or whoever it may have been who booted him out of his God-given superiority and kinghood. Forget him. He's had more promotional work done for him than whole *nations* of better men.

I'm talking about a human need being fulfilled. A small boy wants a dog and finds a dog. A small girl wants a kitten and finds a kitten. A prisoner in solitary confinement has got to have something alive to keep him company through the dreary hours and days and nights, and so he soon makes friends with a cockroach, a mouse, a lizard, a fly, or even a rat. Why shouldn't he? Every living thing has in it that which makes any living thing worthy of love: the breath of life. How misunderstood a rat can be, for instance. How beautiful a common fly can be, if lovingly and carefully noticed. What a miracle of design, wit, speed, grace, and possibly even intelligence a lizard can be.

But I'm not actually thinking about such things. I'm thinking about the short stories of William Sydney Porter, called O. Henry, because each of his stories had in it the *quality* of something lonely and denied that people could make their own—as if O. Henry's writing were the equivalent of a rubber plant in the hall, or a parrot, or a cat, or even something in the human category, a child who might very well be one's own.

The people of America loved O. Henry, and so did I, once I found out what he was up to. Which I did when I read "A Gift of the

Magi"—gad, how cleverly he told his story, concealing behind laughing language a profound love for the great masses of people who are frequently called the little people. O. Henry himself probably never saw a little person unless he happened to see a midget, as I'm sure he did now and then. Perhaps he even wrote about one of them, a group once neglected by writers and dramatists but lately reasonably unneglected. People weren't little to O. Henry unless they *were*, but even then they were little only on the outside.

— William Saroyan, "O What a Man Was O. Henry," in *The Kenyon Review* 29, No. 5 (November 1967): pp. 671–72.

WILLIS WAGER ON WRITERS FROM TWAIN TO JAMES

[Willis Wager has been a professor at New York University, Boston University, and King College in Bristol Tennessee. His publications include *American Literature: A World View* and *From the Hand of Man: A History of the Arts.* In this excerpt, Wager comments on O. Henry's style of writing, seen in its essence in "The Gift of the Magi."]

A special development of the southern or southwestern oral tale or local color story, grafted onto traditions deriving from Irving and Poe, is the work of William Sydney Porter ("O. Henry"), born in Greensboro, North Carolina, in 1862. At the age of twenty, he went to Texas, became a bank teller, and conducted a humorous weekly, *The Rolling Stone.* Sentenced to five years in an Ohio federal penitentiary for embezzlement, he wrote more than a dozen stories that appeared in national magazines; and after his release in 1901 until his death in 1910 he lived in New York City, writing under his pseudonym some three hundred stories, ultimately collected and brought out in thirteen volumes, of which the earliest are *Cabbages and Kings* (1904) and *The Four Million* (1906). About half of his stories deal with incidents in New York, and practically all of them avoid disturbingly problematical aspects of human experience. He did not appreciate his admirers' calling him the "American Maupassant," for he said he had never tried to write anything dirty.

During the first quarter of the present century his popularity sky-rocketed: by 1920 nearly five million copies of his books had been sold in the United States, and deluxe editions of his complete works were being issued and eagerly bought. An annual volume of the best current short fiction has been named in his honor, the "O. Henry Memorial Award Prize Stories"; and many of his works have been adapted for stage, movies, radio, and TV (where the "O. Henry Tele-vision Playhouse" had a long run). The French particularly have prized O. Henry's stories for their compactness, "exactness of mea-sures and proportions" (as Raoul Narcy has phrased it), and avoid-ance of heavy-handed moralizing. Despite their complete innocence of Marxism, they have reached a wide audience in Russia, where sto-ries with the "O. Henry twist" were being as assiduously cultivated by short story writers as, at the same time, in America were stories in the Chekhov manner. Between 1940 and 1955, reprinting rights were granted in twenty different countries. Enthusiasts for O. Henry have pointed out that his contribution—like Poe's—concerns technique as well as content, and that the trick ending, the informal tone, and the calculated use of telling phrases constitutes an "O. Henry style."

— Willis Wager, *American Literature: A World View* (New York: New York University Press, 1968): pp. 164–65.

RICHARD O'CONNOR ON O. HENRY'S FAME WITHOUT FORTUNE

[Richard O'Connor (1915–1975) worked briefly as a Broadway actor before becoming a journalist, a biogra-pher, and a novelist. His publications include *Counter Stroke*, released under the pseudonym Patrick Wayland, and *Winged Legend: The Story of Amelia Earhart*, under the pseudonym John Burke. In this excerpt, O'Connor dis-cusses the unique circumstances leading to the creation of "The Gift of the Magi."]

The *World* had almost as much difficulty in extracting "The Gift of the Magi" from O. Henry as it did any material for its publicity pro-motion. That most famous of his stories—the one invariably included in high-school reading programs—was produced under even more hectic circumstances than usual. His story, reflecting a bachelor's sentimental view of marriage in the extreme devotion of the young husband and wife, but certainly not his own experiences with the complexities of married love, was scheduled for the *Sunday World*'s Christmas issue. It had to have something to do with Christmas, something at least faintly religious, though O. Henry himself was what one of his acquaintances called a sterling example of the "modern world pagan." He wasn't against religion, he simply ignored it.

The *World* decided that O. Henry's Christmas story would form the centerpiece of its magazine section with its illustrations in color. Running the magazine section through the color presses meant that the illustrations had to be ready well in advance of the usual deadline, and that the text of the story also had to be set in type before the rest of the section. A long struggle between the editors under the golden dome on Park Row and O. Henry in Irving Place then ensued. The deadline came and went. Editors agonized and O. Henry comforted them with the usual bland excuses.

Finally Dan Smith, the illustrator assigned to the project, was sent sloshing through the snow to interview O. Henry in his rooms at 55 Irving Place.

Unperturbed, O. Henry admitted to Smith that not a line of the story had been written; worse yet that he hadn't the glimmering of an idea for it.

"I've got to work on the drawings at once," Smith said despairingly. "Can't you tell me something to draw and then fit your story to it?"

O. Henry stared out the window for a few moments and finally told the artist in his Carolinian drawl that he might be able to ad-lib something. "I'll tell you what you do, Colonel," he said, conferring the usual military title on someone he didn't know very well. "Just draw a picture of a poorly furnished room, the kind you find in a boarding house or rooming house over on the West Side. In the room there is only a chair or two, a chest of drawers, a bed, and a trunk. On the bed, a man and a girl are sitting side by side. They are talking about Christmas. The man has a watch fob in his hand. He is playing with it while he is thinking. The girl's principal feature is the long beautiful hair that is hanging down her back. That's all I can think of now. But the story is coming."

—Richard O'Connor, *O. Henry: The Legendary Life of William S. Porter* (New York: Doubleday and Company, 1970): pp. 157–58.

PHILIP STEVNICK ON THE AMERICAN SHORT STORY

[Philip Stevnick became a full professor at Temple University in 1967. His publications include *Alternative Pleasures: Post Realist Fiction and the Tradition*. He was also the editor for the publication *Anti-Story: An Anthology of Experimental Fiction*. In this excerpt, Stevnick talks of the "antireal" notion of plot, noting "The Gift of the Magi" specifically.]

For another viewpoint, there is Leo Marx's brilliant *The Machine in the Garden,* which traces the permutations, through the nineteenth century, of the tension between a bucolic, idyllic, pastoral ideal and the intrusion of the culture of the machine, variously embraced and deplored. It is a tension by no means resolved by the twentieth century, and it suggests the dialectical pattern I have been attempting to describe. Short fiction had had, for a hundred years, a special affinity for the portrayal of a place that is at once the landscape of the mind and the landscape of fact. But in that body of fiction I have sought to portray as counterrealistic, the idyllic is embraced, with sentiment and without reservation. And in that body of fiction we call realistic, the bucolic place is understood, perhaps even loved—frontier farm, wilderness, midwestern town—but not embraced, because no one, writing realistically in the twentieth century, can imagine the happy village, circumscribed, devoid of railroad tracks, factories, and the intrusion of an often meretricious technology.

But finally to return to literary conventions, it is plot, more than anything else, that came to seem antireal. Anderson says it best, and once he has said it and acted upon it, it does not need to be said again, even though there is no writer of significance after him who does not feel it. No segment of life can be said to begin, or end, or resolve itself. Life does not contain plots. The history of short fiction in the first half of the century can be traced, as I have suggested, as a revolt against certain prohibitions and vacuous values; but most of all, it can be traced as a revolt against plot. For the writer seeking to be a realist, the primary imperative, for fifty years, was to avoid making a story look like Maupassant's "The Necklace" or O. Henry's "The Gift of the Magi." For plot, more than anything else, was anti-real. It should be said, of course, that we have come to understand plot in a more fluid and comprehensive way, and those stories that must have seemed devoid of plot when they appeared—Hemingway's "Hills Like White Elephants" for example—seem now to be flawlessly plotted in an unobtrusive and subtle way. Still, it is easy enough to understand what the early writers of the century mean by plot. It is linear and overt, with a crisp beginning, middle, and end, and we recognize the end because it contains an element of surprise.

— Philip Stevnick, *The American Short Story 1900–1945: A Critical History* (Boston: Twayne Publishers, 1984): pp. 14–15.

TRUEMAN E. O'QUINN ON O. HENRY'S UNENDING TRIAL

[Trueman E. O'Quinn collaborated with Jenny Lind Porter in creating a biography on O. Henry's life, focusing primarily on his time in prison, the stories that emerged at that time, and the origin of the pseudonym O. Henry. In this excerpt, O'Quinn claims that the sacrifices made by O. Henry's first wife, Athol, acted as the germ for the story "The Gift of the Magi."]

Frances Goggin Maltby writes in her book *The Dimity Sweetheart* that Will may have first seen Athol at the laying of the cornerstone of the new Capitol in 1885 when Athol represented her class at that ceremony and placed in the cornerstone both class mementoes and one of her long, golden curls. That evening Athol had to iron her ruffled dimity frock again and restyle her hair because a sudden shower had soaked her dress and curls—and she was going to a dance given by the Austin Grays, a militia company which included one Will Porter!

This incident may have been the inspiration of O. Henry's "The Purple Dress."

Will and Athol settled into a small "Honeymoon Cottage" at 505 East Eleventh Street, and they were living there when their newborn son died in 1888 and when their daughter, Margaret Worth Porter, was born September 30, 1889. I purchased this cottage and later made it possible for the City of Austin to acquire it to be made into a youth center in Wooten Park adjacent to Lamar Boulevard, but it was destroyed by a fire set by vandals in 1956. I did save the white pomegranate from the yard at 505 East Eleventh Street (Athol and Will used to place cuttings from this shrub on their little boy's grave), and its "descendants" are alive in my own garden to this day.

From the home on Eleventh Street, Will and Athol moved to 308 East Fourth, across the street from the Roach family. This home was moved to Fifth Street (now the O. Henry Museum), and it was for this cottage that Athol bought muslin curtains and wicker chairs, using the money Will had saved to send her to the World's Fair in Chicago, because she said she loved home and Will more than any trip she could possibly take. Her sacrifice is the source of the celebrated O. Henry story, "The Gift of the Magi," where the young wife Della cuts off her long hair and sells it in order to buy her husband a present. Tuberculosis claimed Athol July 25, 1897, and O. Henry's only child, Margaret, also succumbed to this disease, in 1927, in Banning, California, having been married only a few days to Guy Sartin.

— Trueman E. O'Quinn, "O. Henry's Unending Trial," in *Time to Write: How William Sydney Porter Became O. Henry* (Austin, Texas: Eakin Press, 1986): pp. 7–8.

KAREN CHARMAINE BLANSFIELD ON O. HENRY'S PLOT PATTERNS

[Karen Charmaine Blansfield did an intensive study of the formula contained in O. Henry's stories, which she published in her book entitled *Cheap Rooms and Restless Hearts*. In this excerpt, Blansfield categorizes the plot pattern found in "The Gift of the Magi."]

The plot pattern which Porter employs most frequently, and the one most discussed and referred to by critics, is what can be called the cross pattern. This pattern is characterized by certain specific elements, but because of variations in these elements, it will be further divided into three sub-patterns: cross-purposes, crossed-paths, and cross-identity. In the cross pattern, the surprise ending occurs at the point where two paths travelled by characters in the story intersect, seemingly unexpectedly; however, closer examination reveals that usually this crossing was on the map all along, though so small and remote as to be easily overlooked. This intersection is the significant element in the cross formula, and Porter maneuvers his characters toward it via three separate routes.

The first route is the widely known and discussed pattern of cross-purposes. Here a central problem which induces the entire action of the plot presents itself at the outset. Generally the dilemma is financial, demanding action by one or both of the characters involved, who are united at the story's opening, split to pursue independent paths, and reunite at the close. The core of the plot is this: two characters are simultaneously working to solve some problem, each one unaware of the other's efforts; however, when they unite at the end and discover one another's strategies, it turns out that one individual's actions have in some way affected the other's, with the result usually being that both actions are cancelled out so that the characters have unwittingly been working against, or at cross-purposes to, one another. There are exceptions, though, and the outcome isn't necessarily futile, for the irony of the situation can serve to reinforce the relationship between the two characters.

The story which most vividly illustrates this pattern is also the most well-known of all Porter's tales, "The Gift of the Magi," which James Douglas considers "perhaps the finest tabloid story in literature." Set in an eight-dollar-a-week New York City furnished flat on Christmas Eve day, the story centers around an impoverished young couple surviving on little more than love. Each of these "children," as Porter calls them, has one prize possession which both cherish: Della's long, lustrous hair, and Jim's heirloom gold watch. At the opening, Della is lamenting the insufficiency of the $1.87 she has managed to scrape together for Jim's Christmas present. Struck by sudden inspiration, she rushes out and sells her hair for $20; with the money, she buys Jim a handsome watch fob, then returns home to nervously await his arrival. When he comes and beholds Della's close-cropped curls, he reacts with a kind of shock, the result, one would assume, of his wife's transformation. But the real reason for his astonishment soon becomes apparent; he has bought Della the set of beautiful combs which she had for so long admired in a Broadway window. Della, eagerly insisting that her hair will soon grow back, then presents him with the watch chain, whereupon Jim informs her that he has sold the watch in order to buy the combs.

—Karen Charmaine Blansfield, *Cheap Rooms and Restless Hearts: A Study of Formula in the Urban Tales of William Sydney Porder* (Bowling Green, Ohio: Bowling Green State University Press, 1988): pp. 39–40.

Plot Summary of
"A Municipal Report"

"A Municipal Report," O. Henry's first-person account of a Nashville murder laced with mystery and coincidence, opens with a brief discourse on various American cities. This opening section leads to a statement the story goes on to prove: "It is a rash one who will lay his finger on the map and say: 'In this town there can be no romance—what could happen here?'"

The story begins at 8:00 p.m. in Nashville, Tennessee, just as the "I" narrator steps off the train. The reader is given a brief description of the rainy evening, before the narrator gets into a tumbril (which he mocks adequately) and is driven to his hotel. The narrator's ironic tone continues as he tells of the "renovated" hotel, the southern hospitality of the management, the slow and good-humored service, and the unique cuisine. While at dinner, he asks a waiter about Nashville nightlife, to which the waiter replies that the town closes up after sundown. After dinner, the narrator decides to confirm that the streets truly are deserted.

Throughout the course of the telling, the narrator offers several side bits of information that have some relevance to the city or the story. O. Henry structures these asides by sectioning them off into isolated paragraphs, separated from the story by a space above and below the paragraph. The first aside states a two-line fact about the cost of lighting the streets by electricity.

Following the aside, the narrator takes a walk through the inactive streets. He gives the reader a fairly detailed account of the ordinary situation and eventually returns to his hotel, where the reader and the narrator are introduced to Major Wentworth Caswell. Major Caswell is described as a verbose, British drunk, who instantly becomes the focal point of the narrator's mockery. It does not take long for the Major to acquaint himself with the narrator and drag him to the bar. The narrator describes, with his standard ironic flair, the mundane details of Major Caswell's banter. After buying a round of drinks, the Major speaks loudly of his wife's money, which he uses for his own pleasure. The narrator purchases the next round of drinks to even up the bill and quickly relieves himself of the Major's overbearing company.

As the narrator retrieves his room key from the desk, the clerk asks if he would care to file a complaint about the boisterous Major. The narrator acknowledges that he does not care for the Major's company but declines to make a complaint. He then takes the opportunity to reemphasize his opinion that Nashville is indeed a dull town, asking the fateful question: "What manner of excitement, adventure, or entertainment, have you to offer to the stranger within your gates?" He proceeds to his room where he gazes into the empty streets and restates his impression that Nashville is "a quiet place."

The narrator then addresses the reader directly, suggesting the need to explain the circumstances of his visit to Nashville. The reader is told of Azalea Adair, a contributor to a northern literary magazine for whom the narrator works. It is the narrator's job to get Azalea to sign a contract to release her writing (essays and poems) to the magazine before another publication offers her more.

The action continues the following morning after breakfast, when the narrator leaves the hotel and the reader is introduced to Uncle Caesar, an African-American taxi driver adorned in an incredibly extravagant coat. The narrator describes the coat in great detail, highlighting the one remaining button, which is "the size of a half-dollar, made of yellow horn and sewed on with coarse twine." The narrator enters the taxi and requests to be taken to Azalea Adair's home.

Upon arrival, the narrator offers the appropriate sum of 50 cents to the driver, along with an additional quarter because he is feeling generous. The driver surprisingly protests, claiming that the fee is two dollars. After a brief argument about the price of the ride, during which the narrator claims that he is not some "greenhorn Yankee" but a southerner from not too far away, the driver admits that the fare is indeed 50 cents. He says that in spite of this, he desperately needs two dollars to make up for a general lack of business. Mildly taken by the driver's plea, the narrator offers up the two dollars. As he hands over the bills, he notices that one of them is missing a corner and has been taped together in the middle. He opens the gate and heads into Azalea's house.

The house is a "decayed mansion," providing only a fragile layer of shelter and sorely in need of a paint job. Azalea is a fragile, 50-year-old woman, whose condition is compared directly to the state of her frail home. She greets the narrator with simple cordiality and leads him into the disheveled living room. As Azalea and the narrator converse, the reader is told of the unique process by which Azalea was educated. The reader is also informed of the poor state of her attire and her equally poor financial situation. Taking these factors into consideration, the narrator finds himself incapable of discussing the meager terms of the contract, deciding instead to postpone these talks to the following afternoon. As the narrator heads for the door, he states again that Nashville is a relatively tame town, "where few things out of the ordinary ever happen." After a certain amount of reflection, Azalea makes the loaded comment: "Isn't it in the still, quiet places that things do happen?" This leads to a conversation in which Azalea tells a sophisticated tale, showing the vast range of her mind despite coming from a "hum-drum town."

The story is interrupted by a knock on the back door, and Azalea politely excuses herself to answer. She returns three minutes later looking revitalized, requesting that the narrator stay for tea and a snack. Azalea summons her help, an African-American girl named Impy, and pulls out a ripped dollar bill from her purse, the same bill that the narrator had just given to the taxi driver. Azalea hands it to Impy, instructing her to bring back some tea and sugar cakes. Soon after Impy leaves the room, a scream is heard, along with a man's voice. Azalea leaves the room, only to return a few minutes later to rescind her invitation to tea.

After returning to his hotel, the narrator approaches Uncle Caesar and schedules a ride to Azalea's house for the following afternoon. He inquires about the driver's relationship with Azalea, attempting to determine how the ripped bill traveled out of the driver's possession and into Azalea's purse. Uncle Caesar explains that he had once belonged to her father, Judge Adair. Deciding not to inquire any further, the narrator retreats back to the hotel. He wires his magazine and falsely claims that Azalea is holding out for more money on her contract. The magazine wires him back with instructions to give her what she wants.

Prior to dinner, the narrator goes to the bar, where he is confronted once again by Major Wentworth Caswell. The Major whips out two dollars from his pocket and places them on the bar. Gazing at the bills, the narrator realizes that one of the bills is the same ripped dollar that he had given to the driver and had then seen again in Azalea's hands. Unsure of what to make of the situation, he retires to his room and goes to sleep.

The next day, the narrator takes the taxi to Azalea's house and instructs Uncle Caesar to wait until the meeting is finished. After signing the contact, Azalea slips weakly out of her chair and drops to the floor. The narrator quickly sends Uncle Caesar for a doctor. He returns with Dr. Merriman, who sends Uncle Caesar to his house for some milk and port wine for Azalea. While he is gone, Dr. Merriman tells the narrator about Azalea's impoverished state, adding that she (Mrs. Azalea Adair Caswell) is too proud to accept help from her friends. The narrator is shocked to hear Azalea's last name, realizing for the first time that she is the wife of Major Wentworth Caswell. The doctor confirms that she is indeed married to the drunken Major, confirming that he steals even the small sums of money that the servants provide. On his way out, the doctor also reveals that Uncle Caesar is the grandson of a king.

After the doctor leaves, the narrator gives Azalea a fifty-dollar advance on her contract before returning to the hotel with Uncle Caesar. He goes for a walk that evening and sees Uncle Caesar standing beside his car, looking more disheveled then usual. He also notices that the last remaining button on his coat is now missing. Approximately two hours later, the narrator comes upon a crowd of people standing outside a drugstore. Working his way inside the crowd, he sees the dead body of Major Wentworth Caswell. He discovers that the Major had been found dead in an alley and was brought over to the drugstore. The Major apparently had been involved in a brawl, which he evidently lost. His fists were still clenched tightly together.

Standing next to the corpse, the narrator witnesses the fingers in the Major's right hand relax, dropping a small object beside his foot. He covers the object with his shoe, then picks it up and drops it into his pocket. He concludes that the Major seized the object just before he died.

Later that evening, the narrator sits around a common area of the hotel where people are discussing the murder. He overhears someone say that the Major had been flaunting fifty dollars earlier in the day, though no money had been found on his person.

The narrator leaves Nashville by train the following morning. As the train is "crossing the bridge over the Cumberland River," he reaches into his pocket and takes the "yellow horn overcoat button the size of a fifty-cent piece" (the button that had been missing from Uncle Caesar's coat) out of his pocket and throws it into the river. ❈

List of Characters in
"A Municipal Report"

The "I" narrator is the first character the reader encounters. The "I" is the storyteller, recounting his experience in Nashville, Tennessee, where he was commissioned by a northern literary magazine to sign Azalea Adair, a contributor of essays and poems, to a contract releasing her work to their publication. In the process of meeting Azalea, he realizes that there is a connection between the taxi driver and a drunken British Major, with whom he had had drinks. He eventually finds the Major's dead body lying outside a drugstore. He removes an object from the corpse's hand, which is not revealed until he is on his way home. The object is a button from the taxi driver's coat, indicating to the reader that the driver had killed the Major.

Azalea Adair Caswell is the contributor to the magazine that the narrator works for. She is a frail woman who is being exploited by her husband. It is revealed in the latter half of the story that her husband is Major Wentworth Caswell, the drunkard the narrator has already grown to dislike. It is also revealed that Azalea's family had once owned Uncle Caesar, the narrator's taxi driver. The Major takes the money the narrator gave to Azalea, and the story leads the reader to believe that the driver killed the Major and returned the money to Azalea.

Major Wentworth Caswell is the boisterous British drunkard who loiters around the narrator's hotel and bar. He is the exploitative husband of Azalea Adair who is eventually found dead in front of a drugstore.

Uncle Caesar is the taxi driver who takes the narrator to Azalea Adair's house. He wears an extravagant overcoat with only one button. The narrator learns that he has royal blood and was once owned by Azalea's grandfather. The story's implies that Uncle Caesar killed the Major and returned the money to Azalea.

Dr. Merriman is the doctor who attends Azalea after she faints. He informs the narrator of Uncle Caesar's royal blood, as well as the fact that Azalea is married to Major Caswell.

Impy is Azalea's servant who takes the ripped dollar from Azalea to buy tea and sugar cakes. ❀

Critical Views on
"A Municipal Report"

FRED LEWIS PATTEE ON O. HENRY AND THE HAND-
BOOKS

[Fred Lewis Pattee (1863–1950) was a widely respected educator, editor, critic, and scholar. He spent thirty years
working as a professor at Pennsylvania State University. His
publications include *The Feminine Fifties* and *The First Century of American Literature, 1770–1870*. In this excerpt,
Pattee discusses O. Henry's ability to write for everybody.
He mentions Frank Norris, the man responsible for insti-
gating the writing of "A Municipal Report" (quoted in the
beginning of that story), as one of O. Henry's influences.]

The twelve of his stories which are known to have been written
during this prison period are manifestly apprentice work. They deal
for the most part with adventure in strange regions—the Southwest,
the Southern mountains, and the lands below the Caribbean. They
are for the most part more elaborate in plot, more studiously conventional, than his later work. Curiously enough, his first master
seems to have been Frank Norris, whose parodies and striking
sketches were appearing in the *San Francisco Wave* and other magazines. The "gentle grafter" brand of "tall talk," for instance, impossible on any human lips save on the vaudeville stage, is identical in
the two writers. There are traces, too, of Harte and Kipling, espe-
cially Kipling, but one quickly forgets all influences and all crude-
nesses as one swings into the current of his tales.

From this time on the short story was his profession: he did
nothing else. Released from prison, he drifted in 1902 to New York
City, writing, as the mood or the need was upon him, stories of
South America or the Southwest, or else "gentle grafter" tales from
the materials he had collected in the Ohio penitentiary. Popularity
came suddenly even as it had come to Jack London, and for much
the same reason: his materials were wild and strange and manifestly
first hand. His first story, "Whistling Dick's Christmas Stocking," had
attracted the attention of *McClure's* because of its materials: it was
the story of the Southern tramp migration at the end of the

Northern summer and it was told evidently by one who himself had been a tramp. All that was known of him was rumor: he had been a cowboy, a tramp, perhaps a yeggman, certainly a soldier of fortune in Honduras and South America, and he was writing with strangely graphic pen of his own experiences. The demand for his work came almost exclusively from the new popular magazines of the journalistic type, tremendously alive, up to date, and so thickly spread over the news stands of the world that they could be sold for ten and fifteen cents. One story forced itself into *Harper's* "Editor's Drawer," another into *The Century,* and a third into *The Outlook,* but all the rest had their start in the wood-pulp journals. He wrote, as he once phrased it, for Mr. Everybody. From first to last *Everybody's Magazine* published twenty-two of the tales, *Munsey's* fourteen, *McClure's* ten, *The Cosmopolitan* six, *The American* and *Hampton's* four each, and the rest found lodgment in such periodicals as *Ainslee's, Collier's, The Black Cat,* and *Short Stories.*

— Fred Lewis Pattee, *The Development of the American Short Story: An Historical Survey* (New York: Biblo and Tannen, 1966): pp. 358–59.

Robert H. Davis and Arthur B. Maurice on O. Henry's Dark Hour

[Robert H. Davis (1881–1949) and Arthur B. Maurice collaborated on a compilation of O. Henry's life, his letters, and his work entitled *The Caliph of Bagdad.* In this excerpt, they comment on the insignificance of particular names in some of O. Henry's stories, most notably, "A Municipal Report."]

Of all the characters that figure in the O. Henry stories Jimmy Valentine is by far the most widely known; in fact, he is the only character who by name stands out conspicuously in the long roster. Probably that is largely due to the popularity of the play and the association of Jimmy's name with the play title. It is a peculiarity of the stories that the names of the men and women who figure in them mean nothing or little. Much the same may be said of the short stories of Guy de

Maupassant, with whom O. Henry has so often been compared. In O. Henry's case the exceptions to this rule are few. The name of Frank Goodwin, who is the outstanding figure through the stories of *Cabbages and Kings,* is relatively well remembered, and in the same book the name of "Beelzebub" Blythe has been preserved through sheer force of alliteration. Della of "The Gift of the Magi"; Dulcie of "An Unfinished Story"; Hetty of "The Third Ingredient"; and Nancy of "The Trimmed Lamp" are not entirely forgotten names. But of the hundreds of thousands who have read and reread the O. Henry tales, how many can recall without reference to the printed page the name of the heroine of "A Municipal Report," the heroine of "The Enchanted Profile," the hero of "Mammom and the Archer," or the hero of "The Defeat of the City"?

—Robert H. Davis and Arthur B. Maurice, *The Caliph of Bagdad: Being Arabian Nights Flashes of the Life, Letters, and Work of O. Henry* (New York: D. Appleton and Company, 1931): pp. 145–46.

E. HUDSON LONG ON NEW YORK AND O. HENRY'S SUCCESS

[E. Hudson Long, an established scholar and educator, taught at Baylor University and has written various publications including a biography on O. Henry entitled *O. Henry: The Man and His Work.* In this excerpt taken from that biography, he discusses the declining state of O. Henry's work and his health throughout the last year of his life, indicating "A Municipal Report," written during that year, as his final great work.]

During the last year of his life he was desperately trying to increase his earning power. In March 1910, *Strictly Business* appeared, containing "A Municipal Report," generally look upon as one of his finest creations. This was the last of his books to be published during his lifetime. In addition to his efforts as a playwright and as a novelist, he wrote six stories and two poems which were printed in the magazines in 1910. This task of writing was made still more difficult by frequent occurrences of ill health. He went to Asheville and joined his wife and daughter. Setting up an office on the fifth floor of a Patton Avenue building, he tried to carry on his work, but was unable to accomplish anything important. In November, after suffering a slight relapse, he appeared to be much better, and by March of the following year he was once more in New York. Again he found himself unable to work and for the next month spent most of the time in bed. His nerves were shattered, and he was unable to continue the task which had brought him back to the city.

The writing of a play based on his story "The World and the Door" had to wait. Vainly he strove to get himself in shape. During the last month of his life in New York he became a hermit and, according to Will Irwin, shut himself up and kept the telephone off the hook. Just what happened during these last days before he was carried to the Polyclinic Hospital, nobody really knows, but nine empty whiskey bottles were found under his bed. C. Alphonso Smith states that Gilman Hall had him removed to the hospital, but Dr. Charles Russell Hancock, the physician, declared that Anne Partlan called him to attend O. Henry. At any rate, only the doctor was with him when he died. The *New York Tribune* for June 6, 1910, carried an account of O. Henry's death, attributing the cause to cirrhosis of the liver and quoting the doctor: "His liver was all wrong, his digestion was shattered, his nerves were in a terrible condition, and his heart was too weak to stand the shock." In more than a full column devoted to O. Henry's death, the *New York Times* on the same date printed the doctor's statement that O. Henry, who was conscious at the end, died from a complication of diseases and not from an operation. No operation, indeed, was performed.

—E. Hudson Long, *O. Henry: The Man and His Work* (New York: A. S. Barnes and Company, 1949): pp. 133–34.

EUGENE CURRENT-GARCIA ON O. HENRY'S SOUTHERN LITERARY HERITAGE

[Eugene Current-Garcia is Hargis Professor Emeritus of American Literature at Auburn University. He helped found the *Southern Humanities Review* in 1967 and served as editor and co-editor until 1979. His publications include *What Is the Short Story?* and *American Short Stories Before 1850.* In this excerpt, Garcia explores the significance of O. Henry's southern influence, citing "A Municipal Report" as an important story with a southern setting.]

The fact that Porter seriously intended writing a series of stories on the contemporary South, and even worked out a detailed outline for them, is clear indication of his life-long attachment to the spirit of his native region. Had he lived to carry out his plan, a significant new chapter might possibly have been added both to the annals of Southern literature and to his own literary career; for few writers of his generation were better equipped than he to capture the essential traits of Southern life and character. Like the old Negro hack driver in "A Municipal Report," "He knew; *he knew*; HE KNEW."

Between the publication of "Vereton Villa" in 1896 and "Let Me Feel Your Pulse" in 1910, Porter published about twenty-eight other short stories which are either laid in a Southern setting (exclusive of Texas and the Southwest) or concerned with the activities and inclinations of Southern characters as opposed to those of characters from other backgrounds. Numerically, these stories add up to less than one-tenth of Porter's total output, but they fully establish his claim to a Southern literary heritage. Some of them connect him with the antebellum Southern tall-tale humor tradition; others, with the post-Civil War Southern local-color school; and all of them display the unmistakable characteristics of Southern attitudes, manners, and speech. Close study of Porter's Southern stories with reference to these three points reveals that his methods in them produce a subtle blend of two basic strains in Southern fiction—the frontier strain and the local-color strain; and this blend can be further seen as a dominant characteristic in nearly all the rest of Porter's fiction, particularly in those stories dealing with Texas outlaws and with swindlers, embezzlers, and fugitives from justice. Though few in number, these Southern stories offer an important key to the understanding of his work as a whole.

—Eugene Current-Garcia, *O. Henry (William Sydney Porter)* (Boston: Twayne Publishers, 1965): p. 48.

E. Hudson Long on O. Henry as a Regional Artist

[E. Hudson Long, an established scholar and educator, taught at Baylor University and has published various publications, including a biography on O. Henry entitled *O. Henry: The Man and His Work*. In this excerpt taken from a collection of essays on American literature, Long talks of the inspiration for writing "A Municipal Report."]

Many years later, following a visit to Nashville, Tennessee, where he stayed at the Maxwell House, praising its fine food and service, O. Henry wrote one of his best Southern stories, "A Municipal Report." Showing the peaceful town drowsing under a slow, heavy drizzle, he captures its essence. The old Negro hack driver, loyal and devoted, is a relic of bygone days, while Azalea Adair is a tenderly protected lady of the old regime. By contrast, Major Caswell, degraded and dishonest, represents the type of "professional Southerner" that O. Henry abhorred.

The tale, written to refute a statement by Frank Norris that the only real "story" cities were New York, New Orleans, and San Francisco, proves that such a conventional place as Nashville could equal any other in human interest. Making artistic use of the prosaic quotations from a Rand and McNally atlas, much in the manner of a Greek chorus, O. Henry contrasts the uneventful, material city against his romantic plot. The accurate depiction of background and characters and the reality of narration blend the obvious and mysterious into a convincing, dramatic situation.

There is a profound touch when the old Negro, who had demanded an exorbitant fare, discovers that his passenger is a Southerner:

> "Boss," he said, "fifty cents is right; but I needs two dollars, suh; I'm *obleeged* to have two dollars. I ain't *demandin'* it now, suh; after I knows whar you's from; I'm jus sayin' that I has to have two dollars to-night and business is mighty po."
>
> Peace and confidence settled upon his heavy features. He had been luckier than he had hoped. Instead of having picked up a greenhorn, ignorant of rates, he had come upon an inheritance.
>
> "You confounded old rascal," I said, reaching down to my pocket, "You ought to be turned over to the police."
>
> For the first time I saw him smile. He knew; *he knew;* HE KNEW.

—E. Hudson Long, "O. Henry as a Regional Artist" in *Essays on American Literature* (Durham, North Carolina: Duke University Press, 1967): pp. 230–31. ☙

RICHARD O'CONNOR ON O. HENRY'S REVIEWS

[Richard O'Connor (1915–1975), worked briefly as a Broadway actor before becoming a journalist, a biographer, and a novelist. His publications include *Counter Stroke*, released under the pseudonym Patrick Wayland, and *Winged Legend: The Story of Amelia Earhart*, under the pseudonym John Burke. In this excerpt, O'Connor discusses the mediocre reviews of one of O. Henry's last books published during his lifetime, *Strictly Business*, which ironically included the widely acclaimed story "A Municipal Report."]

But the steam-heated atmosphere of the Chelsea and the "scenery" afforded by the Manhattan skyline didn't revive him either. Nor did the publication of *Strictly Business*, the last collection of short stories to be published in his lifetime. That volume contained more of his New York stories, most of them originally published by the *Sunday World*.

The reviews were lukewarm, though *Strictly Business* included some of his best stories, "The Gold That Glittered," "The Fifth Wheel," "A Municipal Report," "Past One at Rooney's," and "The Poet and the Peasant" among them. The setting of "The Gold That Glittered" was one of his favorite haunts on his night rambles around the Union Square section, the Hotel America on Fifteenth Street, which . . . he called El Refugio in the story. It was the place where Caribbean and South and Central American exiles gathered to plot their return to power, and "The Gold That Glittered" was a lively account of the Americanization of one of those fugitive revolutionaries, General Perrico Ximenes Villablanca Falcon, who "had the mustache of a shooting-gallery proprietor, wore the full dress of a Texas congressman, and had the important aspect of an uninstructed delegate." General Falcon has come to the United States on a gun-running mission but instead falls in love with Mme. O' Brien, the "unimpeachably blonde" proprietor of El Regusio, upon which he concludes that "War and revolution are not nice. It is not best that one shall always follow Minerva. No. It is of quite desirable to keep hotels and be with that Juno—that ox-eyed Juno. Ah! what hair of gold it is that she have!" The story ends with the general's panegyric to Mme. O' Brien's corned-beef hash.

—Richard O' Connor, *O. Henry: The Legendary Life of William S. Porter* (New York: Doubleday and Company, 1970): pp. 224–25. ⊚

C. Alphonso Smith on O. Henry's Favourite Themes

[C. Alphonso Smith (1864–1924) was a North Carolina native who knew O. Henry before his writing career. He was a professor at University of Virginia and at the U.S. Naval Academy in Annapolis. He published the first biography ever written on O. Henry. In this excerpt, Smith discusses the challenge (by Frank Norris) that O. Henry answered in writing "A Municipal Report."]

In "A Municipal Report," O. Henry answers the challenge of Frank Norris who had said:

> Fancy a novel about Chicago or Buffalo, let us say, or Nashville, Tennessee! There are just three big cities in the United States that are "story cities"—New York, of course, New Orleans, and best of the lot, San Francisco.

O. Henry replies:

> But, dear cousins all (from Adam and Eve descended), it is a rash one who will lay his finger on the map and say: "In this town there can be no romance—what could happen here?" Yes, it is a bold and a rash deed to challenge in one sentence history, romance, and Rand and McNally.

Then follows a story of Nashville, Tennessee, which O. Henry had visited when his daughter was attending Belmont College. "For me," writes Mr. Albert Frederick Wilson, of New York University, "it is the finest example of the short story ever produced in America." "If the reader is not satisfied," says Mr. Stephen Leacock, after attempting to summarize "Jeff Peters as a Personal Magnet" and "The Furnished Room," "let him procure for himself the story called 'A Municipal Report' in the volume 'Strictly Business.' After he has read it he will either pronounce O. Henry one of the greatest masters of modern fiction or else, well, or else he is a jackass. Let us put it that way."

The story ends on the note with which it began: "I wonder what's doing in Buffalo?" It is O. Henry's most powerful presentation of his conviction that to the seeing eye all cities are story cities. It is the appeal of an interpretative genius from statistics to life, from the husks of a municipality as gathered by Rand and McNally to the heart of a city as seen by an artist.

—C. Alphonso Smith, *O. Henry* (New York: Chelsea House Publishers, 1980): pp. 230–31.

EUGENE CURRENT-GARCIA ON O. HENRY'S SOUTHERN TIES

[Eugene Current-Garcia is Hargis Professor Emeritus of American Literature at Auburn University. He helped found the *Southern Humanities Review* in 1967 and served as editor and co-editor until 1979. His publications include *What Is the Short Story?* and *American Short Stories Before 1850*. In this excerpt, Garcia discusses the "authorial self-assurance" of the narrative voice in "A Municipal Report."]

"Blind Man's Holiday" is a hopelessly idealized mélange based on the hackneyed theme of noble self-sacrifice and strung out woodenly to a moralistic harangue quite untypical of O. Henry's later work. For serious students of his career its main interest may reside in his treatment of guilt feelings suffered over a shadowed past—an obvious parallel with his own painful history. But today's average reader can only view the story quizzically as a period piece, a study in outmoded taste as well as in its author's groping experimentation with fictional autobiography.

In "A Municipal Report," however, authorial self-assurance is brashly evident from beginning to end. This may be why the story is still regarded as one of O. Henry's finest, although it scarcely deserves the extravagant critical acclaim it received in the 1920s. Several glaring excrescences mar its unity and thus weaken its impact. Economy is sacrificed, for example, in O. Henry's overuse of posturing tricks to build up his narrator's character as an ironic foil for the three other participants in the action: old Caesar, the faithful black coachman and hero; Major Caswell, the villainous white leech; and the starving, genteel author, Azalea Adair. After opening with quoted passages from Kipling and Norris, the narrator interposes two wisecracking paragraphs about cities as a basis for his thematic idea that it is rash to deny the possibility of romance in any given one, large or small. He follows these with a Rand-McNally thumbnail sketch of Nashville and more wisecracks about its limitations as he checks in at a hotel, dines, steps out to look over the somnolent little city where nothing ever happens after sundown, and finally encounters Caswell, the southern bore. In this leisurely way the story drifts on a few more pages—one-third its full length—with more chamber-of-commerce tidbits dropped in now and again before the narrator reveals his primary mission in Nashville as the agent of a northern literary magazine with a contract for Miss Adair. From this point on it does fulfill O. Henry's stated purpose, moving swiftly toward his climax and muted denouement to refute Norris's reckless supposition. But here as elsewhere O. Henry's mastery of picturesque dialect and sharp descriptive detail is clearly superior to his analysis of complex character in action.

—Eugene Current-Garcia, *O. Henry: A Study of the Short Fiction* (New York: Twayne Publishers, 1993): pp. 14–15.

Plot Summary of
"The Furnished Room"

"The Furnished Room" opens with a description of the transient lifestyle of the dwellers of the "red brick district of the lower West side" of Manhattan. The story suggests that a number of these inhabitants are entertainers, living for weeks at a time in a particular apartment before moving on. "Hence the houses of this district, having had a thousand dwellers, should have a thousand tales to tell."

The story begins with a young man arriving in the evening, luggage in hand, wanting to rent a room for a week residency. He approaches a particular building, rings the bell, and is greeted by a housekeeper described as having a "furry" voice. The woman leads the man up a dingy set of stairs—stairs that are described in great detail before the narration reaches the vacant room.

The housekeeper shows the room, offering a brief history of past tenants, most of whom are affiliated with the entertainment industry. The young man pays for a week and asks the housekeeper about a particular girl, Miss Eloise Vashner, the very girl whom he has asked about on countless other occasions; the girl he once loved; the girl responsible for his transient lifestyle. In describing her to the housekeeper, he mentions her fair skin, the color of her hair, her height, and the dark mole near her left eyebrow. The housekeeper claims that she is unfamiliar with the particular name, repeating the fact that people come and go all the time.

The reader is then informed that the man has searched for this girl, his lost love, for the past five months: "So much time spent by day in questioning managers, agents, schools and choruses; by night among the audiences of theaters from all-star casts down to music halls."

The focus then shifts to the "furnished room." The room is largely personified by the narrative, acting almost as a character, offering "pseudo-hospitality," and a "perfunctory welcome like the specious smile of a demirep," while also appearing to be "confused in speech." The reader is then taken on a narrative tour of the apartment, which includes the worn condition of the furniture, the "gay-papered" wall, and the random articles left behind by past tenants.

Following the tour, the man sits back in a reclining chair and attempts to uncover information about past tenants based on the particular objects that appear around him. He scrutinizes every article like a detective searching for clues, in an effort to re-create the history of the room. He takes in the "furnished sounds and furnished scents" that rise around him. He becomes keenly aware of every element inside and outside the room, absorbing all into his meandering mind. At this point he is struck by the familiar smell of mignonette.

The fragrance is so potent that he responds audibly to its presence, asking: "'What dear?' as if he had been called." His senses become helplessly intertwined, leading him to recognize the fragrance as a vocal presence. He exclaims aloud: "she has been in this room," initiating his search for any remnant of his lost love. He tears apart drawers and dressers, smelling and touching every article that he encounters. He moves on to the walls and corners of the room, crawling around the floor and searching for any sign or scent. He feels her presence calling him from inside the room. His senses are rich with her essence.

He continues his search, allowing nothing to elude his desperate eyes. After scouring every inch of the room, he seeks out the housekeeper again to inquire more specifically about the prior tenants. The woman offers a fairly detailed account of the past year's occupants, answering multiple questions about each, yet revealing nothing of substance. The man thanks her and retreats to the furnished room.

Upon his return, he finds a complete absence of any fragrance or feeling of her presence. The room is suddenly lifeless. He stares helplessly at the gaslight before walking to his bed and ripping the bed sheet into multiple strips. With the edge of his knife, he wedges the strips into every opening in the apartment. When the apartment is completely sealed, he flips off the light, turns the gas on high, and lays down on his bed to die.

The narrative then shifts to a conversation between the housekeeper, Mrs. Purdy, and her friend Mrs. McCool. Mrs. Purdy explains to her friend that she had rented the third floor room to a young man earlier in the day. Mrs. McCool asks whether she had informed the man of the suicide that had taken place last week. She admits that she had not, leading Mrs. McCool to disclose the details of how the young lady had lay in bed and killed herself with gas. The story ends with Mrs. Purdy commenting on the attractive appearance of the young girl, "but for that mole she had a-growin' by her left eyebrow," making it clear to the reader, that the girl the man had been searching for, his lost love, had died in an identical manner, in the same room, only a week before. Yet another example of the O. Henry surprise ending. ❀

List of Characters in
"The Furnished Room"

The young man is the first character the reader encounters. He takes a room in a lower West side apartment building, inhabited almost exclusively by transients. He has spent the past five months searching for his lost love. He recognizes a fragrance worn by her and proceeds to scour the room for clues. After asking the housekeeper about the tenants who had inhabited his room prior to himself and finding no useful information, he returns to his room and commits suicide.

Mrs. Purdy is the housekeeper who rents the room to the young man. She conceals the fact that there had been a suicide in that particular room only a week earlier. It is revealed in her conversation at the end that it was the young man's lost love who had committed suicide.

Mrs. McCool is Mrs. Purdy's friend. It is in her conversation with Mrs. Purdy, the final scene in the story, when the reader discovers that the young man's lost love had committed suicide.

Miss Eloise Vashner is the young man's lost love. Although she does not appear in the story, the possibility of her presence is what drives the narrative. The ladies reveal in the end that Eloise had committed suicide in the same fashion and in the same room as the young man. ❀

Critical Views on
"The Furnished Room"

ROBERT H. DAVIS AND ARTHUR B. MAURICE ON THE
WIDE APPEAL OF O. HENRY

[Robert H. Davis (1881–1949) and Arthur B. Maurice collaborated on a compilation of O. Henry's life, his letters,
and his work entitled *The Caliph of Bagdad*. In this excerpt,
they discuss the particular appeal and quality of "The Furnished Room."]

It is significant that Leacock, Adcock, and De Kobra have all singled
out one story to be placed above all the rest. That is not "A Municipal Report" or "An Unfinished Story," which most Americans are
likely to mention first, but "The Furnished Room." Of that tale
Stephen Leacock said: "It shows O. Henry at his best as a master of
that supreme pathos that springs, with but little adventitious aid of
time or circumstance, from the fundamental things of life itself. In
the sheer art of narration there is nothing done by Maupassant that
surpasses 'The Furnished Room.'" St. John Adcock singled out the
story to echo Professor Leacock's appreciation. In Paris one day
some winters ago M. De Kobra and Arthur Maurice indulged in an
O. Henry "fanning bee." "Which one do you like best?" was asked.
"The Furnished Room," was the Frenchman's instant reply. "And
after that?" "The Gift of the Magi."

Which one do you like best? The question suggests one very extra-
ordinary aspect of the O. Henry appeal. That so many persons differ as
to their favorites among his tales is the finest possible tribute to the
edifice that he built in the span of his brief working life. To illustrate
the point in the simple and most direct way, suppose symposiums, or
plebiscites, or what you will, were held to find out which were the
most popular stories of Maupassant, Stevenson, Poe, Kipling, and Bret
Harte. It would be fairly easy to guess at the general result.

—Robert H. Davis and Arthur B. Maurice. *The Caliph of Bagdad:
Being Arabian Nights Flashes of the Life, Letters, and Work of O. Henry*
(New York: D. Appleton and Company, 1931): pp. 375–76.

George F. Whicher on the Spokesman of the Plain People

[George F. Whicher, a scholar of American literature, has contributed his research and writings to various publications, including the extensive material on twentieth-century literature which was published in the comprehensive volume entitled *The Literature of the American People: An Historical and Critical Survey*. In this excerpt, Whicher mentions "The Furnished Room" as an example of O. Henry's ability to produce multiple stories containing only a slight difference in theme.]

The short story in the hands of William Sydney Porter (1862–1910), who always signed his work "O. Henry," lent itself easily to ingeniously contrived plots and to the investing of commonplace people and places with a factitious glamour. Porter, born in North Carolina, went to Texas at twenty, worked in a bank, and started a humorous weekly. Charged with embezzlement of a small sum of money, he fled to Honduras, but returned to stand trial when he heard that his wife was dying. A period for reflection afforded by a three-year jail sentence changed him from a writer of humorous anecdotes to an artist in the devising of clever fiction. From 1902 till the end of his life he poured out a rapid succession of stories, enough to fill fourteen volumes when his works were collected. His popularity was as brief as his performance.

O. Henry's first book, *Cabbages and Kings*, which appeared in 1904, is made up of loosely connected stories dealing with adventurers adrift in a Latin America where revolutions are taken lightly as part of the day's work. On occasion he also wrote narratives with a Southern or Southwestern setting. His most characteristic vein, however, was opened with *The Four Million* (1906), made up of tales that purport to reveal the unsuspected romance in the lives of humdrum people living in New York. O. Henry's characters are never subtle or significant. His effects depend largely on circumstances neatly manipulated to produce an ironic or an unforeseen ending and on a running fire of smart comment and witty badinage spoken by the author. An O. Henry story always has the air of being told in a barroom.

He was inexhaustibly fertile in producing variations on a few simple themes and plot formulas. No philosophic grasp of life was required. All he needed was a free hand to contrive coincidences and cross accidents. In "The Gift of the Magi" a young husband sells his choicest possession, a fine watch, to buy his wife a set of combs to wear in her beautiful hair; the wife meanwhile sells her hair to pay for a chain to go with the husband's watch. In "The Furnished Room" a girl from the country, defeated in her hope to become a singer, commits suicide in her cheap lodgings; a little later a young man who loves her and is desperately trying to find her rents the same room, and maddened by the faint smell of mignonette, her perfume, he also kills himself. For a third example, in "Soapy" a tramp commits several intentional misdemeanors in order to get himself a comfortable jail sentence for the winter months, but through the perversity of fate he always fails to get himself arrested. He drifts on to a church, where the sound of religious music awakens a flickering resolve to lead a better life, and at that moment he is collared as a vagrant.

O. Henry could and did go on and on with this sort of thing. There has never been a better demonstration of the essential emptiness of mechanical novelty. Nor can one praise the running fire of wisecracks with which he adorned his narratives. But as a popular entertainer he adapted the short story to a more extended and democratic audience than it had ever previously known. A certain cheapening of the form was implicit in the process. Not more than a dozen of his stories at most are memorable. His success made it impossible for those who came after him to take pride in the mere commercial production of short stories. The only direction of advance was toward greater artistic integrity.

—George F. Whicher, "Spokesman of the Plain People," in *The Literature of the American People: An Historical and Critical Survey* (New York: Meredith Corporation, 1951): pp. 837–38.

Van Wyck Brooks and Otto L. Bettmann on O. Henry's Storytelling Skills

[Van Wyck Brooks (1886–1963) and Otto L. Bettmann combined their talents to create a pictorial history of the

American writer. Brooks was an editor and critic whose publications include *Sketches in Criticism* (1932) and *Emerson and Others* (1927). Bettmann was an active member of the American Federation of the Arts. His publications include *The New Pictorial Encyclopedia of the World* (1954). In this excerpt, they discuss the skill with which O. Henry captured the image in "The Furnished Room."]

He never ceased to be surprised by the wonders of a city where something was always happening round the corner. A piano-player in a cheap café might have shot lions in Africa, a bell-boy might have fought with the British against the Zulus, and O. Henry knew of an expressman who had been rescued from a cannibal feast when his arm was crushed for the stew-pot like the claw of a lobster. For the rest, in O. Henry's vision, the city was a quicksand. It shifted its particles constantly; it had no foundation. Its upper granules of today were buried tomorrow in ooze and slime, and mysteries followed one another closely in a town where men vanished like the flame of a candle that has been blown out.

O. Henry had a special feeling, even at times an incomparable feeling, for the sad milieu that he pictured in "The Furnished Room." With what skill he described the ragged brocade of the chipped bruised chairs and the broken couch, distorted by bursting springs, the shredded matting that bulged in the rank sunless air. Over and over he told the stories of the girls whose parlour was the street-corner and whose garden-walk was the park. They dreamed of a bungalow on the shores of Long Island or a home in Flatbush. Whatever their fate, they remained inviolate and mistress of themselves.

With his brisk and often too obvious stories, O. Henry was occasionally an artist who escaped from the mechanical formulas of the cheap magazines, the last to vindicate Howells' belief that the "more smiling aspects of life" were the most characteristic of America, as no doubt they had been.

—Van Wyck Brooks and Otto L. Bettmann, *Our Literary Heritage: A Pictorial History of the Writer in America* (New York: E. F. Dutton and Company, 1956): p. 189.

[Gilbert Millstein is a journalist whose feature articles have appeared in various publications, including the *New York Times Magazine*. In this excerpt, Millstein discusses O. Henry's intimate knowledge of New York, seen quite vividly in the interior description contained in the story "The Furnished Room."]

The distaste harbored by the old rich for the new and the resentment of the latter for the former were well understood, in all their fatuity, by O. Henry and he disposed of them in a few reasonably good-natured lines: "Old Anthony Rockwell, retired manufacturer and proprietor of Rockwell's Eureka soap, looked out the library window of his Fifth Avenue mansion and grinned. His neighbor to the right—the aristocratic clubman, G. Van Schuylight Suffolk-Jones—came out to his waiting motor-car, wrinkling a contumelious nostril, as usual, at the Italian Renaissance sculpture of the soap palace's elevation.

"'Stuck-up old statuette of nothing doing,' commented the ex-Soap King. 'The Eden Musée'll get that old frozen Nesselrode yet if he don't watch out. I'll have this house painted red, white, and blue, next summer and see if that'll make his Dutch nose turn up any higher.'" Upon being informed later, by his refined, second-generation-rich son that money "won't buy one into the exclusive circles of society," the old man dismisses the young man with, "You tell me where your exclusive circles would be if the first Astor hadn't had the money to pay for his steerage passage over."

He was intimately acquainted with "those decaying but venerable old red-brick mansions in the West Twenties"; the middle-class flat "paved with Parian marble in the entrance hall and cobblestones above the first floor" and the furnishings, "1903 antique upholstered parlor set, oil chromo of geishas in a Harlem tea house, rubber plant and husband"; the dismal furnished room in Chelsea with its "decayed furniture, the ragged brocade upholstery of a couch and two chairs, a foot-wide cheap pier glass between the two windows . . . a brass bedstead," and its occupant, certain to be one of that band of people "restless, shifting, fugacious as time itself," "transients in abode, transients in heart and mind," ineffably sad; the "Brickdust Row" of the very poor, lighted by "the yellow, singing gaslight."

—Gilbert Millstein, "O. Henry's New Yorkers—And Today's" in *The New York Times Magazine* (September 1962): pp. 134–35.

Roman Samarin on O. Henry's Remarkable Writing Ability

[Roman Samarin is a Soviet literary scholar who has contributed to various publications, including *The Soviet Review,* a journal consisting entirely of translated material. In this excerpt, Samarin argues against the critical claim that O. Henry sugarcoats his endings. The story "The Furnished Room" can be considered in support of Samarin's argument.]

Some critics say that O. Henry saw in art a means of creating soothing illusions; they refer to his "Last Leaf" as a case in point. A girl artist, dying of pneumonia, luckless, untalented but sweet, apathetically awaits the day when the last leaf falls from the old ivy vine climbing up the wall opposite her window. The doctor had given her to understand she would live no longer than that. . . . The days pass, but the leaf keeps glowing in its bright autumn colors against the dreary gray of the brick wall. The girl conquers her disease. We know, however, that the leaf she has been gazing at was not the one that had long been blown away by the autumn wind, but the one that had been skillfully painted on the wall by the old artist living downstairs. His art had saved her life. That is the power of illusion, you might say: the real purpose of art is gently and wisely to delude and soothe the suffering heart.

But the old artist paid a price for saving the girl. He contracted pneumonia during the cold wet night he had pained his masterpiece, and died. Consequently, the meaning of art lies not in creating an illusion, but in serving man, as the forsaken artist showed. There was a moment in his life when he was really great— because he saved another.

In serving man and fulfilling the writer's duties as he understood them, O. Henry drew a broad panorama of American life at the turn of our century, leaving behind him a unique portrait gallery of American types of his time.

The Big City in his panorama stands aggressively in the fore. He once remarked that he had written of the things the giant city had whispered, trumpeted and shouted to him. In his short stories you can hear that music: the blatant voices of hired newspaper writers and advertising agencies that shape the minds of the philistines, the bawling of hard-boiled politicians and demagogues, the whispers and complaints of those who have been dumped to the bottom of society or are docilely dragging out a drab existence in the hope of somehow making ends meet. O. Henry's stories often mention those vain naive hopes, the dreams that never come true. Even if they do, the very incredibility of the fact only confirms the illusory quality of the dreams.

—Roman Samarin, "O. Henry—'A Really Remarkable Writer'" in *The Soviet Review* 3, No. 12 (December 1962): pp. 55–56.

David Stuart on O. Henry's People

[David Stuart is a literary scholar whose publications include an extensive biography dedicated solely to the life of William Sydney Porter. In this excerpt, Stuart focuses on the events that lead to the writing of "The Furnished Room."]

He would go anywhere that seemed to suggest a story. One evening he found one right at home. He had, as was so usual with him, spent all the money advanced for his most recent literary effort and was "dead broke." He worked all afternoon and into the evening, unable to afford to go out to dinner. Until the story was finished, and delivered, he could not expect any more money.

The evening wore on. Hunger stilled his pen. He got up and went out into the corridor and walked up and down. He passed a doorway from which emanated the marvelous odor of someone's cooking. He went down the hall, came back and passed the door again. This time, the door opened and a young woman came into the doorway.

"Have you had your supper?" she asked. "I've made a Hazlett stew and it's too much for me. It won't keep, so come and help me eat it."

So O. Henry gratefully went into the girl's room and ate the stew. They talked about feather curling. That was her profession in the big city, curling feathers with a dull blade for the hats of wealthy women.

They talked about life in the city. O. Henry asked what was in the stew and the girl told him, all that she had been able to afford: liver, kidney, and heart of calf.

No matter, it had saved O. Henry that night. He went back to his room and finished his tale. A few days later, rich in pocket, he rapped on the girl's door, intending to reciprocate, no, not reciprocate, but reward her a dozen times by buying her the finest dinner in New York. But the girl was gone. Gone where? No one knew. The city had claimed another victim. That experience coupled with his own imagination, provided O. Henry with the idea for one of his tales of the young woman in the heartless city: "The Furnished Room."

—David Stuart, O. Henry: A Biography of William Sydney Porter
(Chelsea, Michigan: Scarborough House Publishers, 1990): p. 141.

EUGENE CURRENT-GARCIA ON O. HENRY'S FULFILL-MENT IN MANHATTAN

[Eugene Current-Garcia is Hargis Professor Emeritus of American Literature at Auburn University. He helped found the *Southern Humanities Review* in 1967 and served as editor and co-editor until 1979. His publications include *What Is the Short Story?* and *American Short Stories Before 1850*. In this excerpt, Garcia talks about "The Furnished Room" as a story that sheds light on the suffering that rises out of a materialistic society.]

There are at least two opposing ways to interpret O. Henry's fictional treatment of the working class New Yorkers in the early 1900s, and his Russian admirers, as well as many others, seem to have followed both at different times. From one viewpoint these stories may be regarded as an implied, if not an obvious criticism, of the gross inequalities in America's capitalist society; hence this withering jeremiad from the Soviet only thirty years ago: "He gave a general idea of the absurdity of the system under which dire poverty was the source of the amassing of fantastic wealth, and under which the rich became slaves of their millions and lost all human semblance. For O. Henry they were leeches who sucked their capital out of the poor, to whom they paid a pittance so that they might keep body and soul together and help the rich make their millions." But from an opposite viewpoint—also Russian—the stories may be disdained for offering a complacent, if sometimes cynical, approval of the status quo, and their author condemned for his falseness, hypocrisy, and sentimentality—for being, indeed, "the great consoler," a slave to middle-class secular ideals, illusions, and false hopes.

By arguing from a selected assortment of O. Henry's stories, one might have made out a plausible case for either view as recently as the 1960s, but neither would be likely to survive even casual scrutiny today. One might argue, for example, that two of his most popular tales, "The Gift of the Magi" and "The Furnished Room," convey a scathing indictment of the inequities that cause great suffering in America's materialistic society, or one might turn instead to such stories as "The Shocks of Doom," "One Thousand Dollars," or "A Night in New Arabia" to find evidence of O. Henry's loyal support of the ultraconservative doctrine favoring the concentration of wealth in the right hands. But to evaluate his stories from this economic perspective is to endow him with socioeconomic or political philosophic biases he seldom, if ever, expressed. For although he was a sincere humanitarian in his sympathetic gestures toward the poor and downtrodden, as a writer of fiction his outlook was neither that of such realists as Twain and Crane nor that of naturalists such as Norris and Dreiser; his view of the human predicament as seen in the nation's greatest city was consistently that of the romanticist, not unlike Irving's. His most percipient biographer sums it up neatly in three sentences: "His half-dozen Jewish characters, for example, are superficial types, revealing no serious interest in the impact which New York had on the Jewish immigrant. Nor does he show an interest in one of the crucial issues of his day, the growing fight between capital and labor. Aside from his sentimental and somewhat ambivalent concern for the underpaid shopgirl, Porter's interest in New York was that of the perennial tourist."

—Eugene Current-Garcia, *O. Henry: A Study of the Short Fiction* (New York: Twayne Publishers, 1993): pp. 63–64.

Works by
O. Henry

Cabbages and Kings. 1904.

The Four Million. 1906.

The Trimmed Lamp. 1907.

Heart of the West. 1907.

The Voice of the City. 1908.

The Gentle Grafter. 1908.

Roads of Destiny. 1909.

Options. 1909.

Strictly Business. 1910.

Whirligigs. 1910.

Sixes and Sevens. 1911.

Rolling Stones. 1912.

Waifs and Strays. 1917.

The Complete Writings of O. Henry. 1917.

O. Henryana. 1920.

Postscripts. 1923.

The Biographical Edition. 1929.

O. Henry Encore. 1936.

The Complete Works of O. Henry. 1953.

Works about
O. Henry

Adcock, J. St. John. "O. Henry." *Bookman* (1916): 153–57.

Arnett, Ethel Stephens. *O. Henry From Polecat Creek*. Greensboro: Piedmont Press, 1962.

Barban, Arnold M. "The Discovery of an O. Henry Rolling Stone." *American Literature* 31 (1959): 340–41.

Boyd, David. "O. Henry's Road of Destiny." *Americana* 31 (1937): 579–608.

Brown, Deming. "O. Henry in Russia." *Russian Review* 12 (1953): 253–58.

Cesare, Margaret Porter. "My O. Henry," *Mentor* 11 (1923): 17–20.

Clarkson, Paul S. "A Decomposition of Cabbages and Kings." *American Literature* 7 (1935): 195–202.

Courney, L. W. "O. Henry's Case Reconsidered." *American Literature* 14 (1943): 361–71.

Davis, Robert H., and Arthur B. Maurice. *The Caliph of Bagdad*. New York: D. Appleton and Company, 1931.

Echols, Edward C. "O. Henry's 'Shaker of the Attic Salt.'" *Classical Journal* 43 (1948): 488–89.

————. "O. Henry and the Classics—II." *Classical Journal* 44 (1949): 209–10.

Forman, H. J. "O. Henry's Short Stories." *North American Review* 187 (1908): 781–83.

Gallegly, J. S. "Backgrounds and Patterns of O. Henry's Texas Badman Stories." *Rice Institute Pamphlet* 42 (1955): 1–32.

Gates, William B. "O. Henry and Shakespeare." *Shakespeare Association Bulletin* 19 (1944): 20–25.

Gohdes, Clarence. "Some Letters by O. Henry." *South Atlantic Quarterly* 38 (1939): 31–39.

Henderson, Archibald. "O. Henry—A Contemporary Classic." *South Atlantic Quarterly* 22 (1923): 270–78.

Jennings, Al. *Through the Shadows With O. Henry*. London: Duckworth and Company, 1923.

Jung, Margetta. "O. Henry in Manhattan." *Southwest Review* 24 (1939): 410–15.

Kercheville, F. M. "O. Henry and Don Alphonso." *New Mexico Quarterly Review* 1 (1931): 367–88.

Leacock, Stephen. "O. Henry and His Critics." *New Republic* 9 (1916): 120–22.

Lomax, J. A. "Henry Steger and O. Henry." *Southwest Review* 24 (1939): 299–316.

Maltby, Frances G. *The Dimity Sweetheart*. Richmond: Dietz Printing Company, 1930.

McAllister, Dan. "Negligently, Perhaps; Criminally, Never." *South Atlantic Quarterly* 51 (1952): 562–73.

Narcy, Raoul. "O. Henry Through French Eyes." *Living Age* 303 (1919): 86–88.

Newbolt, Frank. "Letter to a Dead Author." *Nineteenth Century* 82 (1917): 825–34.

O'Quinn, Trueman. "O. Henry in Austin." *Southwest Historical Quarterly* 43 (1939): 143–57.

Page, A. W. "Little Pictures of O. Henry." *Bookman* 37 (1913): 381–87.

Pattee, Fred Lewis. "The Journalization of American Literature." *Unpopular Review* 7 (1917): 374–94.

Payne, L. W., Jr. "The Humor of O. Henry." *Texas Review* 4 (1918): 18–37.

Peck, H. T. "The American Story Teller." *Bookman* 31 (1910).

Richardson, C. F. "O. Henry and New Orleans." *Bookman* 39 (1914): 281–87.

Robinson, Duncan. "O. Henry's Austin." *Southwest Review* 24 (1939): 388–410.

Rollins, Hyder E. "O. Henry." *Sewanee Review* 22 (1914): 213–32.

Samarin, Roman. "O. Henry—'A Really Remarkable Writer.'" *Soviet Review* (1962): 55–58.

Sinclair, Upton. *Bill Porter: A Drama of O. Henry in Prison*. Pasadena: Published by the Author, 1925.

Smith, C. Alphonso. *O. Henry Biography*. New York: Doubleday, Page and Company, 1916.

Steger, H. P. "O. Henry: New Facts About the Great Author." *Cosmopolitan* 53 (1912): 655–63.

Travis, Edmunds. "O. Henry's Austin Years." *Bunker's Monthly* (1928): 493–508.

Van Doren, Carl. "O. Henry." *Texas Review* 2 (1917): 248–59.

Williams, William Wash. *The Quiet Lodger of Irving Place*. New York: E. P. Dutton and Company, 1936.

Index of
Themes and Ideas